No Love; Lost.

Tyler Lewis

1

Table of Contents

Section I - Eros & Ludus

First Sight   13
6th Sense   14
A New Feeling   15
Primary Attraction   16
Love Theatrics   17
Relations   18
Intimacy   19
Muse   20
Table for 2   21
Love Language   22
Lost For Words   23
Irresistible Force   24
Ode to My First Love   25
Ransom   26
Fleeting Memories   27

Section II - Mania

Mixed Emotions	31
Beautiful Disaster	32
Puzzling	33
Hand In Hand	34
Last Time	35
In The End	36
Truth Hurts	37
Family Ties	38
Running Outta Time	39
No Air	40
Expiration	41
Crossroads	42
Parts of a Whole	43
If I Knew	44
No Love; Lost	45

Section III - Pragma & Philautia

Our Untold Story   49
Before The World Ends…   50
Solace & Serenity   51
Girls Need Love   52
Fated Encounter   53
Vitality   54
The Full Picture   55
And I Wonder…   56
By The Weekend (Die With You)   57
All I Want   58
Something Special   59
Home Is Where The Heart Is   60
Ode to my Posterity   61
The Older I Get   62
Through It All   63

To my younger self

Section I - Eros & Ludus

First Sight

Eyes met before words,
Hearts matched before anything.
Love from just a glance.

6th Sense

Give me a chance to truly see you,
let me know it all; every part
that causes me to falter
my actions whenever
you utter my name,
my heart cannot
wait to meet
all of
you.

A New Feeling

Look me in the eyes,
Tell me how you feel.

My walls are down,
Vulnerable to your truths.

Gently caress my soul
As I lose myself in your presence.

Me and you,
Here and now.

Let's embrace this moment
Like it's our first and last.

Primary Attraction

You removed my shades,
Opening me up to hues
The moment we met.

Love Theatrics

I'm yearning to be close to you
Again, in your blissful presence.

Your smooth chocolate curves
Swirled with my sweet caramel,

A stolen glance from you
Is all it takes to paint me red.

I'm full of embarrassment
At the sight of your beauty,

She knows no bounds and
I am shaking at the pressure.

I can't take any more chances,
I'm itching to see you again.

Relations

Deep breaths, idle thoughts as time passes
where we lay bare and entangled
while the sunrise kisses on
our skin drenched in sweat
with us intertwined;
As the day stands
still, we sit
in the
now.

Intimacy

I can lower my guard with you,
Tell you my innermost thoughts.

Can you hear them?

Screaming at me to love you,
All of you.
I promise that I won't falter.

I find solace in your company
And serenity in your love.

Press your skin unto mine,
Sense my yearn for you.

Can you feel it?

Draw me closer,
Lose ourselves in intimacy.

Muse

You're the reason I stay awake at night,
I always get lost in your eyes.

They tell me a thousand stories
But I rather hear them from your lips.

Serenade me with your beauty,
I am forever at your mercy.

Skin dipped in honey and gold,
Painted over your curvaceous canvas.

You're the epitome of a Goddess,
Fluent in the language of divine love.

My heart only knows what it wants
And it yearns for your wisdom.

You emit energy that's so rare, so pure,
It's no wonder my world revolves around you.

Table For 2

I take the finer things in life for granted,
With you being one of them.

I never knew what elegance meant
Until I caught a glimpse of your beauty.

Let me wine and dine you the right way,
Take you out for a night on the town.

I want to feel close to you,
To be all up in your space.

Will you allow me to take your hand?
Let me lead you down the path of true love.

Love Languages

Her lips spoke several languages,
They fluently told me what love is.

Lost For Words

Words lack the true intentions of my heart
to where my mere actions escape my clutch.
I am in constant thought, lost at the sight
of your enchanting bliss. A work of art
that beguiles me with an innocent touch
from your eyes to my soul. Throughout the night,
I sing sweet nothings in hopes that they find
you by the time I find the words with such
poise; these are ramblings that last a fortnight.
I give you my all even if ill-timed
despite fright.

Irresistible Force

Is it premature to say I have it all figured out
Or am I just enthralled by your presence?

Not even a trace of angst besieges me
As I embark on this endeavor through your eyes.

Unshaken by the seldom snag or hitch,
My road will always lead back to your heart.

I can get lost with your forever and a day
For I stand firmly in my feelings for you.

I will follow you, eternally fueled by ardor
Venturing into the future we always spoke of.

Ode to My First Love

At first, your love was all I knew.
I couldn't look between the lines,
I locked the doors and shut the blinds,
For my heart yearned only for you.

All we shared were stolen glances,
A secret language all our own.
I dare not seek another tone,
My love can't take any chances.

As we pluck each flower petal,
We dreamed of forever, always.
I wished to see those fateful days
Where my romance doesn't settle.

The end was near and we could tell,
My heart laid bare for all to see,
You longed for the day to be free,
But I guess I did just as well.

Ransom

I am in possession of your heart.
As it beats beautiful life into you,
I will not just stand by and watch.
Even if it takes you eons
I will always be here,
Holding all your love for ransom.

Fleeting Memories

I long for those late nights
With you right beside me,

Gazing upon the stars
That I see in your eyes.

We smoked and we laughed
And we talked and we kissed,

Emanating sparks which kept
Us warm under the night sky.

The moon watched over us
As we begun to lose ourselves

To the beat of our own music;
No one could stop our rhythm.

The soundwaves took us off-track
And I forgot why I felt so absent:

Because I'm now just a memory,
A thought that doesn't seem to last forever.

Section II - Mania

Mixed Emotions

I lose myself in your love,
It's so intoxicating to the point
It hurts whenever I can't see you.
Admitting this, it's difficult but
You can't blame me for wanting this,
I never noticed it before but
It's your beauty who's at fault.
I never noticed it before but
You can't blame me for wanting this,
Admitting this, it's difficult but
It hurts whenever I can't see you.
It's so intoxicating to the point
I lose myself in your love.

Beautiful Disaster

I'm writing a song about you today,
I'm sure it's things you've heard before.
Sweet nothings is all I ever wrote.
A soothing baritone to caress your soul,
Something I couldn't achieve.

I wrote a song about you yesterday.
The moon watched over me,
Wading me through the pain I hid so deep.
But this isn't about me it's about you,
It's always about you.

I'll write a song about you tomorrow,
Exposing the truth behind it all.
Laying down notes on the page.
I call it a beautiful disaster,
The best music is always called that.

Hand in Hand

It was just by happenstance that we met,
We couldn't see the doors that can't close once opened.
So we lay there, full of temptation and unanswered questions.

Our late-night conversations ran through morning
And group outings turned to date nights, but
It was just by happenstance that we met.

Our roads diverged but we didn't want to let go.
So we chose a path, walking hand in hand, yet
We couldn't see the doors that can't close once opened.

We were comfortable in each other's arms, but I
Always pondered whether the bed we made was enough.
So we lay there, full of temptation and unanswered questions.

<u>The Last Time</u>

I can't remember the last time I felt your touch,
But then, maybe I shouldn't.

In The End...

I got caught up and we both know it.
Entanglements just turn into unnecessary knots.

I dug my own grave and attempted to bury my emotions,
There's no use in trying to avoid the aftermath.

Can't help but face the fact that I can't face the music.
I walk on a thin line to the beat of my own drum.

Revel at the sight of what was bound to happen;
Past pain can do numbers on a person.

And in the end, all I know is "better".
And in the end, what better lesson to learn?

Truth Hurts

It's hard for me to admit my mistakes,
Wasting your time was one of them.

Every night I fell back into your arms,
It was safe there and I loved it.

You accepted me, my flaws and all,
And I rejected the idea of a future.

What kind of man am I?
That I can't keep a single promise?

All you wanted was a safe space
And all I did was ruin it.

I wish I could rewind the time once more,
I can't help but wonder if I'll stay the course.

We've had our fun in the sun,
But our fifteen minutes of fame is over.

Family Ties

I pleaded my love for her,
Hoping she would feel the same
And alas, she did but like
A little brother.

Running Outta Time

As the clock struck midnight,
I'm stuck splitting hairs
As the roads diverged
Past the moonlit sky.

I stand and lay bare
As the clock struck midnight,
Drawn to temptation,
Allured by contentment.

Windows are closing,
Doors are almost shut.
As the clock struck midnight,
Running outta time.

With a choice to face
And a move to make,
I'm stuck splitting hairs
As the clock struck midnight.

No Air

You have me in a chokehold;
Gasping for air as I suffocate,
Losing myself in your embrace.

Expiration

We never lost track of time,
It plotted against us from the start.
We never stood a chance.

The sun starts setting on us
As the sand trickles down the hourglass,
Too naive to notice the change.

The seconds pass us by,
Getting harder to escape this dream.
Counting down the days till we let go.

Crossroads

I struck a deal with the devil.
He split my heart in two,
Buried them at a crossroads,
Forcing me to dig deep.

We crossed paths after
I struck a deal with the devil,
And I saw the fork in the road
To which my torn heart diverged.

One led down memory lane,
The other was uncharted, and as
I struck a deal with the devil,
I wasn't aware of how much it could hurt.

As I stand before this great divide,
With my heart still split in two,
Fate left me to fend for myself because
I struck a deal with the devil.

Parts Of A Whole

I wanted you for myself.
I thought I needed you close,
Making us parts of a whole
That needs connection.

If I Knew

If I knew then what I know now,
Which strings ache your gentle heart,
Which words were better left unsaid,
I wouldn't need memories of you.

I wouldn't feel the past haunting me
If I knew then what I know now.
If I were present, in the moment,
I would've seen you left long ago.

I would've seen the signals you sent,
Your signs showing me the way,
If I knew then what I know now,
I could've kept this ship going.

I could've shown more of my love,
More of the man you once endeared.
Can I right all the wrongs I've made
If I knew then what I know now?

No Love Lost

We're too far gone now.
We played our parts well
From the moment we locked eyes.
Our hearts enveloped,
Souls were tied,
Connected by thoughts of romance.
As we sit in this moment together,
We saw our future unfold.
We realized no love was lost nor found.
We saw our future unfold
As we sit in this moment together.
Connected by thoughts of romance,
Souls were tied,
Our hearts enveloped.
From the moment we locked eyes,
We played our parts well.
We're too far gone now.

Section III - Pragma & Philautia

Our Untold Story

Are my words,
That weaves lifetimes
And utters old fables,
Grasping your heartstrings?
Jerking your sweet tears?
And will my silk voice
Ever caress your soul
As much as a story foretold?

You show me worlds,
That weaves lifetimes
 And heartens labels,
Can thread fate's strings.
Not even the slightest tear
Coerces my unwavering choice.
As I am but part of the whole
Of our imminent story foretold.

Before The World Ends ...

I wish I could give you those dreams,
Where the cosmos meets at its seems
And stars align your fate,
Shooting for yearnful desires
Before the world sets to expire,
Before it is too late.

After it is all said and done,
After the minute hand has spun
And the clock struck the last hour,
Longing for your innermost thoughts
To scream at me to tie loose knots,
With hope this love is ours.

Solace & Serenity

Let your hair breathe
While you bask in your solace,
Enamored by the sun's kisses.

I know you need this moment,
This peace of mind.
Life always asks too much of you.

Sip your wine and
Take some time.
Nobody can step to you
Right now,
You're Free.

Girls Need Love

I know you have more important things that need your focus. "Us"
Can always take a backseat to finding yourself. Self-
Love works better when your thoughts coincide. Side
With me on this: do you need a reason to keep searching baby? Be
The peace you're trying so hard to look for, Or
You can come find me to help you along the way. A
Man should know when his presence is vital. All
Of this is solely up to you. You
Do what you need to do 'cause girls need love too.

Fated Encounter

First impressions were never a strong suit -
awkward
Our stage was vast, seeking connection that ran off-course -
adrift
Your words sung to me as if met in a past life -
before
Melodies never truly resonated with me until that day -
we met
Two souls that embody a true work of art -
twin flames

Vitality

What does your soul look like to you?
Calm, midnight blue
Or forest green?
Somewhere between?

A soul is like a reflection.
Ask your questions,
Align yourself,
Enrich your health.

Cherish it like you would flowers;
By the hours.
Slowly it grows
And blooms meadows.

The Full Picture

You spilled out your innermost thoughts
To me, hoping you would have caught
One of the few nice guys
Who doesn't combat your affairs
And needs to do more than his share
Without batting an eye.

But to your surprise, I was not
Of the same image that you'd sought
Out for me to portray.
Because I love myself too much
To be seduced by looks and touch
And submit to your ways.

And I Wonder

Have you ever wondered how we got here?
How you steadily take my breath away
With every glance compelling me to stay
By your side and embrace you with care –
Have you ever wondered how we got here?

Mere words cannot help me display
The boundless love I'm yearning to convey
To your heart that's so pure and so rare,
Have you ever wondered how we got here?

Your smile effortlessly brightens my day
As you caress my soul along the way
And I can't help but to keep asking for years,
Have you ever wondered how we got here?

By The Weekend (Die With You)

Let's take down the government, together.
No longer will we be codependent
On the handouts of the corrupt.

Woke up this morning from a nightmare.

Let's smash the patriarchy and beat the system,
Face society head-on like it's the new norm.
Together nothing can stop us.

Looked to my left and you were right there.

Let's break that wretched glass ceiling.
Close the gap and ascend to power,
No one can stop you from ruling the world.

No one is here, we are alone with our love.

Let's move forward and never look back.
Even if the world ends,

I think I wanna die with you.

So take, smash, and break it all to pieces,
Let's do it by the weekend.

All I Want

I want to carry your burdens,
Give me your worries, your fears,
Put it all on my shoulders.

I want you to talk my ear off.
Vent to me about your work,
Spill the tea on your messy friends.

I want you to throw your stress away.
I'll handle all the dirty work for you,
Release you from all that extra waste.

All I want is to bring you peace.

Something Special

It wasn't my intention to make you feel ordinary.
I let something special slip through my hands,
Now all we have left are these fragments of each other.

I grew accustomed to holding a place in your heart,
Which led to me holding my tongue on our love.
It wasn't my intention to make you feel ordinary.

Tunnel vision caused this ship to crash ashore.
Instead of sailing towards what we destined,
I let something special slip through my hands.

Even though we moved beyond our troubled past,
Some pieces can't help but be swept under the rug, and
Now all we have left are these fragments of each other.

Home Is Where The Heart Is

I've always been about you.
Living in my heart rent-free,
No one occupies my space like you.

Come to me whenever you need.
I'll exempt you from taxing labor,
We always leave work at the door.

Let loose as soon as you walk in.
Throw away routine and unwind.
With me, you're always home.

Ode to My Posterity

As days go by and months run long,
I mourn the thoughts of my mistakes.
I then knew not to tempt my fate
Because she loves to prove me wrong.

You live within my heart for now,
But one day you'll be in my arms;
Protecting you from any harm
And loving you, that is my vow.

O, you innocent girl or boy,
My worries run deeper than seas.
The apple falls close to the tree
And I knew to be nothing but coy.

Who knew that you would be the one
To make me understand true love?
The kind you just can't get rid of,
The kind that burns just like the sun.

Please accept me as I am and
I pray that your love won't falter.
A boy with love of a father,
Awaiting for your day so grand.

The Older I Get

I'm finding happiness the older I get.
In what the future may hold for me,
With the present bringing serenity,
How the past forced me to face regret,
I'm finding happiness the older I get.

Slowly realizing what it means to face reality,
To move with the intent of bringing harmony
In everything I do and haven't done yet,
I'm finding happiness the older I get.

Until life can feel more like a fantasy
Where the stars guide me towards your galaxy,
Forever changing this solo to a duet,
I'm finding happiness the older I get.

Through It All

Before this life ends,
And after all the lessons,
All that's left is you.

About The Author

Tyler Lewis is an African American writer and filmmaker born and raised in Brooklyn, New York. A creative force from an early age, Tyler began crafting words as a high school student, exploring poetry, novels, and screenplays to express his unique perspective. His passion for storytelling led him through years of refining his craft, experimenting with various mediums to connect with audiences.

No Love; Lost. marks his debut as a published author, showcasing his ability to weave raw emotion and intricate narratives into a compelling first body of work.

Acknowledgments

This journey has been six years in the making, filled with countless moments of overthinking, stress, and doubt. But through it all, I couldn't have reached this point without the unwavering support of my incredible community. Honestly, without each of you, I'm not sure I'd be here today, sharing this moment with you.

First and foremost, I must thank my love, Amy. If not for you, I would have given up long ago. Your constant encouragement and belief in me pushed me to keep going, even when I wanted to quit. Your support was as crucial to this book coming to life as my own. Thank you from the bottom of my heart.

A huge thank you to my mother, Denise, for not only helping to finance this project but for being my rock every step of the way. You've always shown me what it means to keep moving forward, no matter the challenges. Your unconditional support has made it possible for me to chase my dreams. I am forever grateful.

I'd like to express my gratitude to Brendan, who has been my go-to creative partner. Whether I needed an honest critique or help to refine my work, you were always there to provide valuable feedback. Your honesty and insight made this book better in so many ways.

A heartfelt thank you to my publisher and her team, especially Natalie. If it weren't for you, I'm not sure I would have ever had the courage to pursue writing. You've been more than just a publisher—you've been a true mentor, and I look forward to continuing to learn from you. I'm also incredibly grateful to Addison for the time, care, and expertise you've poured into making this project something I'm so proud of.

Finally, to my friends and family—thank you for your endless encouragement. Your belief in me has been a driving force, and I'm forever thankful for your unwavering support. A special shout-out to Ashli, Julia, Isaiah, Adriana, Arianna, Antonia, Latoya, La'Shance, Mizani, Deja, Kenya, and Taiye for always cheering me on.

This book is as much yours as it is mine. Thank you all for being part of this journey.

Made in the USA
Columbia, SC
21 February 2025

54157816R00037